> *Friends* are the most *important* part of your life. Treasure the *tears*, treasure the *laughter*, but most importantly treasure the *memories*.

David Brenner

> You're only here for a short visit. Don't *hurry*, don't *worry* and be sure to *smell* the flowers along the way.

Walter Hagan

A note from Jess

If you were to ask me, who is my best friend? I'd tell you, my best friend is my Nan. She's 60 odd years older than me, but there's no one who "gets" me more than she does.

I'm so lucky to spend every day with my special person. To be able to share the joy that Nan brings our family on a daily basis, with millions of people around the world through social media has been nothing short of incredible.

Nan has shown me nothing other than unconditional love, security, safety and happiness throughout my whole life. She is an inspiration to many and I can only hope I become even half the woman she is.

I've had the chance to ask her all the questions I've ever dreamed to know, and record so many special memories together. I'll treasure these moments for the rest of my life.

This book is dedicated to the thousands of people who have left us messages saying how special our relationship is and how much it reminds them of times they shared with their loved ones.

We hope this book brings you closer to a special person in your life. Cherish it in this lifetime and gift it to generations to come.

Whatever your story, there's magic in every chapter.

Treasure this,
Jess

> You have to be *unique* and *different* and *shine* in your own way.

Lady Gaga

A note from Norma

As I sit here reflecting on my life, I am overwhelmed with emotion. From the earliest memories of childhood to the bittersweetness of growing older, to the unbelievable last few years we've had on social media, my cup is so full.

I've been blessed with my family, who show me endless love: my wonderful children, Kate and my son, and my beautiful grandchildren, Jessica and Cadan. I love them all dearly.

Jess has always had a special place in my heart. Her laughter echoing through the house, her energy filling every corner with life. She has brought joy into my life, even during the toughest times.

There may be decades between us, but she's my best friend. We have a remarkable time, don't we, together? It just works.

We've laughed, we've cried, we've faced the world and the shower (the "torture chamber", we joke) hand in hand. As long as we have each other, I know that everything will be okay.

I love you Jess, my dear granddaughter, my light in the darkness, my heart.

This book is for the moments we've shared, and the ones yet to come. It's to be filled with laughter and love, tales of family and friendship.

I hope everyone reading this scribbles down their stories and makes this book thick with photos and keepsakes. Your story is your gift. Use this book to share it with someone who holds a special place in your heart, like my Jess.

The kind letters and great support we've received from people from all four corners of the globe has brought me so much joy. Thank you.

These truly are the golden years.

Treasure this,
Norma

Jess holding brother Cadan, 2003.

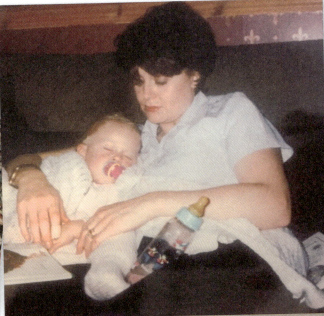

Jess with mum Kate, 1996.

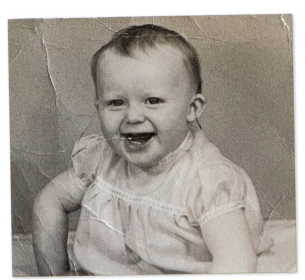

Mum Kate on her first birthday, 23rd May 1969.

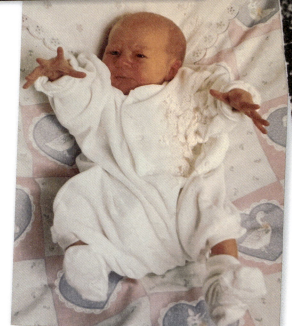

Jess 1996.

Now, let me share some of *my* memories with *you*...

ITV Interview, April 2023.

Above: Grandad Michael, Nostell Priory, May 1961.
Left: Norma and her mum Jessie at Skegness Beach, roughly 1938.

Left to Right: Jessie (Norma's Mum), Joan (Norma's Sister) and Betty (Norma's Sister). Taken at Norma's wedding, 1962.

Let's start at the beginning.

My family, though small, has always been my world.

Thinking back to my early years, my sisters, my mother —they were the foundation upon which I built my life.

We were three girls, just a family of three girls with my mum. My dad died when I was seven. My oldest sister was 16 years older than me, and she was a teacher. Betty was the middle one, there were nine years between Betty and I. But we were on the same wavelength. I miss them both very much.

My mum, bless her. She died of cancer when I was 34. I can't tell you how lovely she was. When you hugged her, her face was so soft. She always smelled of talcum powder. You don't forget those things. She worked hard to keep us together through the war. Every deed she did was for the family. She's been gone more than 50 years now and I still miss her.

Growing up during the war, I learned resilience and gratitude.

I was five years old when war broke out. I can remember little things like the siren going off warning an air raid. Your tummy would sink. We got under the table, wondering if we could be hit. I can remember walking down to school in the morning with my gas mask on my shoulder. Those masks were incredible things, but awful things - I can still smell the rubber. Putting them on was so frightening as a child, it made you feel like something imminent was looming.

Every now and then we'd practise for an air raid at school. We'd have to go into the Anderson bomb shelters. I can smell the damp and the wet cement, even now. I can still feel the cold. We were very lucky where we lived. We practised, but we never experienced an air raid.

Norma and her friends at the Telephone Exchange, 1952.

> Passing my final exam to become a GPO trained telephonist. What a proud moment.

I was 17, and I loved it. I loved that job. The girls I worked with were wonderful people and they still are. We meet once about every five weeks for lunch. Over the years we've lost several of them along the way. Now I am the oldest one at our meetings.

After I was married and the children had gone to school, I worked at the local primary school looking after the children during dinnertime. I loved those kids. They were lovely. I'm very thankful I did that because the school still has a very special place in my heart. It has. I was there for years, and finally left at 59 because my deafness had increased and it was making it difficult for me.

My late husband, bless his soul, was a pillar of strength and love.

Christmas Eve, 1960. That was a different Christmas, because I met Michael. We were married in '62.

He had a wonderful gift for making things from wood, unbelievable things. Everyone in the family has a bit of Michael's art. He looked after us and he made certain that I wanted for nothing. He may have been quiet, but his presence spoke volumes.

I remember he used to stand in the bathroom with Jessica, teaching her how to wash her hands. He used to say, "you must go right down each finger". Little things like that. They don't leave you. They're there.

He's been gone 20 years, which feels almost as if… did it happen? I have to grab back the memories of my life with him and I have some beautiful memories, but they seem so distant now.

He may have left us physically, but his spirit lives on in every corner of our home.

Norma and Michael's wedding, 27th August 1962.

Norma and Michael at Jess' Mum Kate's wedding, 1992.

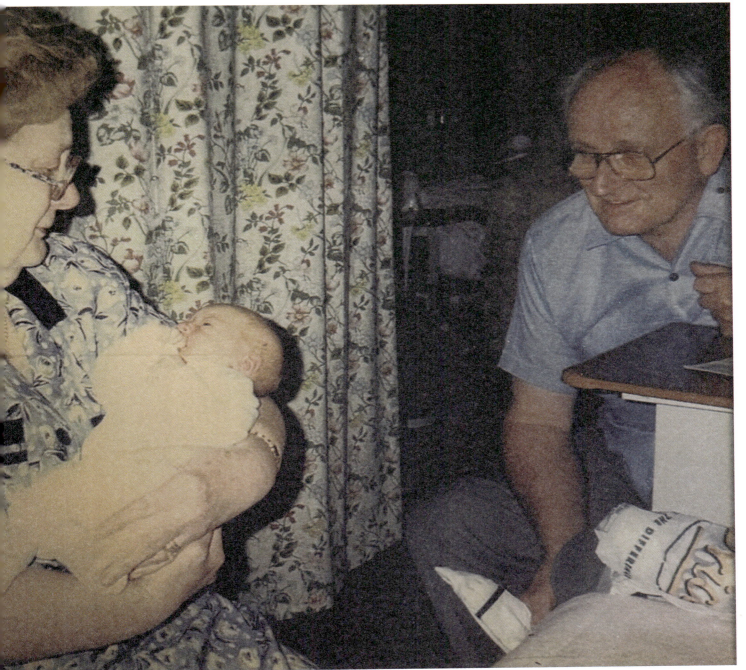

Norma and Michael meeting Jess, 8th June 1996.

> *So much of my life was focussed on family over anything else.*

For me, family is first, it's everything. I've been blessed with wonderful children and two grandchildren who I love more than anything.

The experience of raising my two children and then being so lucky to become a grandparent - I've enjoyed every minute of it. It hasn't been easy at times, but then, it never is. I just loved being there to look after them. I think the people at work thought I was mad because I said I liked it when the kids were off from school so I could look after them. And that's true. It really is.

I did go abroad a couple of times in my twenties, but I never went abroad again. Michael and I bought a caravan, piled in the family and went up to Northumberland for holidays. It was lovely. We appreciated the simple things in life.

Family visit to Cleethorpes, 2023.

Jess, 2000.

And then there's Jess, my rock, my light.

I remember those "Mickey Mouse" stories I used to tell Jessica. They weren't about the Disney Mickey Mouse, each one was a little world of its own, filled with characters and lessons. It was our ritual, me sitting at the edge of her bed, Jess wide-eyed with wonder as I spun tales of Bluey, Smokey, and Squeaky. She'd walk through the front door and shout, "Mickey Mouse!". I used to look at my husband and say, "I haven't got another one ready yet!" I still cherish those moments.

Life hasn't always been this easy, Jess has had her struggles, feelings of fear, uncertainty and anxiety. We went through some very difficult times. I can remember as a child she would not let Michael open the front door when we were leaving the house, we never found out exactly why.

As an adult, we have now had some answers that explain the whirlwind of emotions and energy that defined her childhood. Thankfully things are much brighter now. She's found her Jake and I couldn't wish for her to be with anyone better.

She brings laughter into my life every day and brought us - by accident - into this world of social media. It was all a bit odd at first because we didn't really know where it could lead or what could happen. I was a bit scared in a way. But I've found a new sense of purpose in the most unlikely of places. It's been fun. It's kept me going. At this age, I didn't want to be pushed into a corner and forgotten... with my crossword.

Now, having recently celebrated my 90th birthday, I find myself filled with gratitude for the life I've lived, for the love I've shared, for the memories that sustain me. And though the world may change around us, one thing remains constant - our family bond, unbreakable and everlasting.

My advice?

Don't lose touch with your family. Go through life, work as hard as you can. Have fun and stay well. I think nobody could wish for more, really.

Now it's time to write *your* story...

THE LIFE STORY OF

_____

_____

shared with

_____

_____

Family Tree

This is a scrapbook page to create your very own family tree.

Tell me where it all began, when and where you were born. Tell me about your parents, grandparents, siblings and children.

All families are different, so with this book you'll find stickers ready to fill in and then stick onto this tree.

Put yourself in the middle of the tree, add older generations above and younger generations below.

Use this page to add notes about your Family Tree.

When and where were people born? What did they do for work? Did they get married?

Scrapbook Page

Use this page to record memories by sticking in photos, boarding passes, special ribbons, flowers etc.

Tell me your earliest memory.

Why do you think it stuck with you?

This or that...
Tea or Coffee?

Describe a special place from your childhood.

What does it mean to you?

Tell me about mealtimes growing up

What foods bring back special memories?

This or that...

Beach or Mountains?

Are there any special bedtime stories or routines you remember?

Scrapbook Page

Use this page to record memories by sticking in photos, boarding passes, special ribbons, flowers etc.

Did you have any unusual or quirky traits when you were younger?

This or that...

Cats or Dogs?

Tell me about your closest friends over the years.

How did you celebrate holidays or special occasions when you were growing up?

This or that...

Summer or Winter?

What were your aspirations or dreams when you were younger, and did you fulfil them?

Quick fire questions

What's something you've always wanted to learn but never had the chance to?

What's the strangest or most adventurous thing you've ever eaten?

Is there a skill or talent you possess that might surprise people?

If you could choose any career path besides the one you pursued, what would it be?

If you could witness any event in history, what would it be and why?

What's the most surprising or unexpected gift you've ever received?

Tell me about your proudest moments.

This or that...

Morning Person or Night Owl?

If you could relive one moment from your past, which would it be and why?

Is there a particular place you've visited over the years that left a lasting impression on you?

This or that...
Sweet or Savoury?

Tell me about your most memorable holidays over the years.

Scrapbook Page

Use this page to record memories by sticking in photos, boarding passes, special ribbons, flowers etc.

Where did you party when you were younger?

This or that...

Books or Movies?

What's the most daring thing you've ever done in your life?

How did you feel before, during and afterwards?

Tell me about your signature scents?

Any perfumes or aftershaves you used to wear over the years? What is your favourite now? Do any scents remind you of a specific memory?

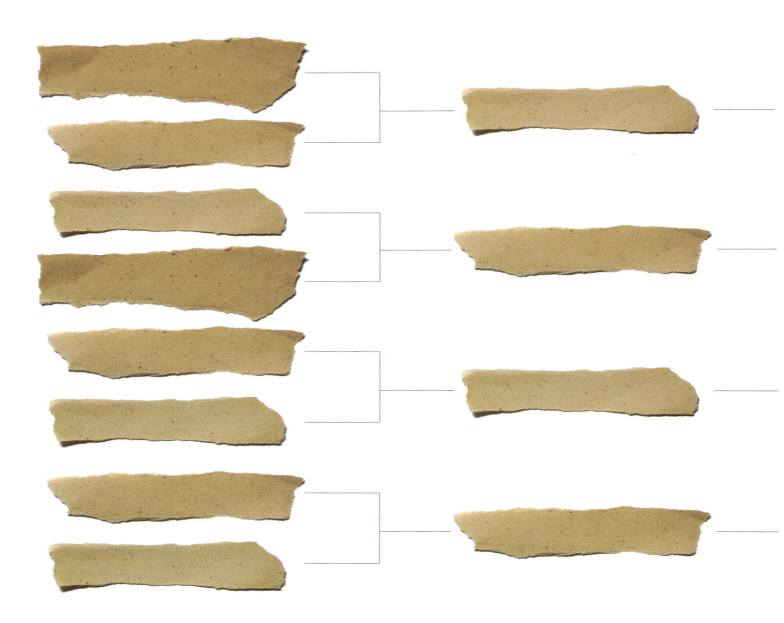

My anthem

Tell me your favourite songs, we'll do knockout rounds until we land on the anthem to your life.

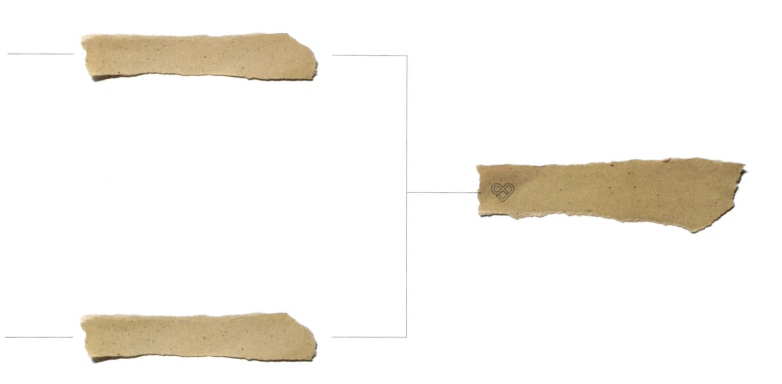

What historical events do you remember most vividly from your lifetime?

This or that...
City or Countryside?

How did you meet your spouse/partner?

Tell me about some of your most treasured memories with them.

Let's talk about your favourite toys.

Tell me about any toys you played with growing up. Did you have any favourites? Were there any toys you really wanted that you couldn't have? Do you still have any?

Scrapbook Page

Use this page to record memories by sticking in photos, boarding passes, special ribbons, flowers etc.

What do you remember most strongly about your work life?

This or that...

Introvert or Extrovert?

Can you recall any significant challenges you faced in your life, and how you overcame them?

Tell me about a turning point that changed your life forever.

This or that...
Sunrise or Sunset?

Between me and
you... share a secret.

Scrapbook Page

Use this page to record memories by sticking in photos, boarding passes, special ribbons, flowers etc.

Do you have any regrets?

This or that...

*Phone Call or
Text Message?*

What's something you've always wanted to do but have been too afraid to try?

Is there a dream or aspiration you've given up on because you didn't believe in yourself?

This or that...
Chocolate or Vanilla?

You're hosting the ultimate dinner party, which 5 guests are invited - dead or alive?

Quick fire questions

Who was your first kiss?

Have you ever had a brush with fame or encountered a celebrity?

What jobs were common in your childhood that don't exist today?

What's your favourite fashion trend of all time?

What's your favourite flower?

What's your favourite colour?

What's still left on your bucket list?

This or that...

Rainy Day or Sunny Day?

What are some valuable life lessons you've learned that you'd like to pass on?

What do you hope your legacy will be for future generations?

This or that...
Comedy or Drama?

100 years from now, how would you like to be remembered?

This or that...

Home Cooking or Dining Out?

Scrapbook Page

Use this page to record memories by sticking in photos, boarding passes, special ribbons, flowers etc.

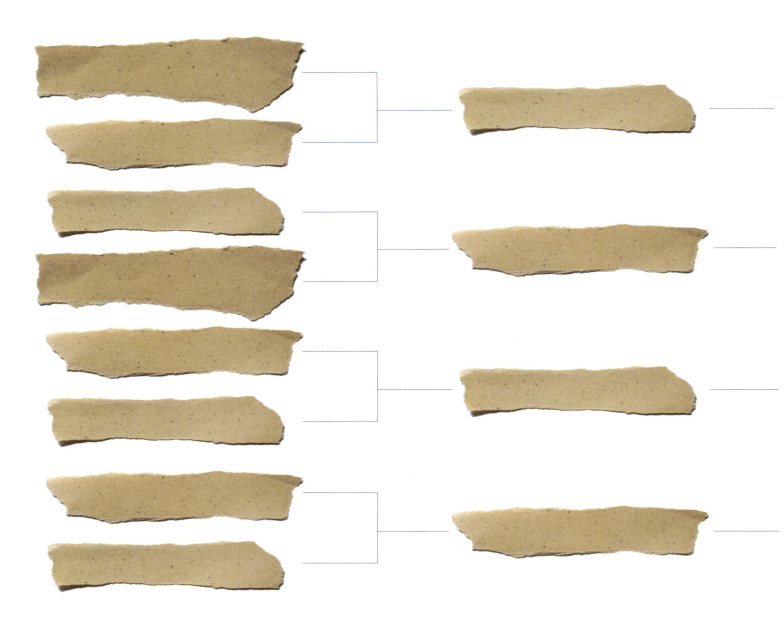

Movies that stole my heart

Tell me your favourite movies, we'll do knockout rounds until we land on your all time favourite.

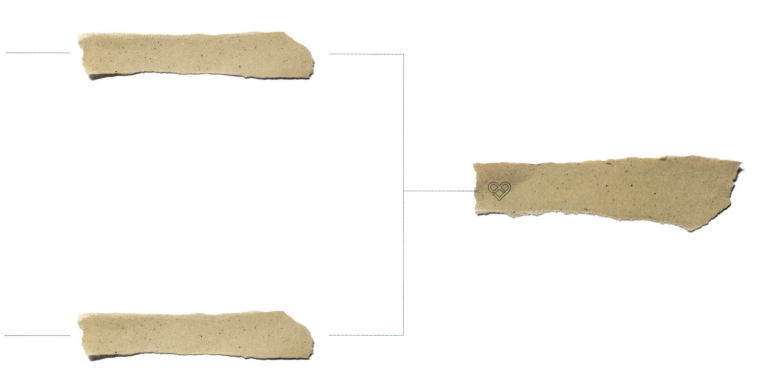

Handprint

Put your hand on the page
and I'll draw around it.

 Your Hand

My Hand

Memory brain dump

Use these pages to record more memories, old and new.

119

A note to treasure forever

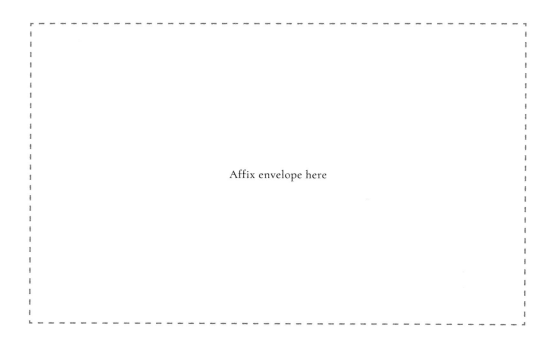

Affix envelope here